South West Coast Path
Somerset & North Devon Coast

Minehead to Bude

GN00578078

Part of the England Coast Path

Text: *Dennis and Jan Kelsall*
Series editor: *Tony Bowerman*
Photographs: *Dennis and Jan Kelsall, Alamy, Adobe Stock, Dreamstime, Shutterstock*

Design: *Carl Rogers and Laura Hodgkinson*

© *Northern Eye Books Limited 2019*

Dennis and Jan Kelsall have asserted their rights under the Copyright, Designs and Patents Act, 1988 to be identified as the author of this work. All rights reserved.

This book contains mapping data licensed from the Ordnance Survey with the permission of the Controller of Her Majesty's Stationery Office. © Crown copyright 2019. All rights reserved. License number 100047867.

Northern Eye Books

ISBN 978-1-908632-73-9

A CIP catalogue record for this book is available from the British Library.

Printed and bound in the UK.

www.northerneyebooks.co.uk

Cover: *Clovelly harbour at dusk (Walk 6)*

Important Advice: The routes described in this book are undertaken at the reader's own risk. Walkers should take into account their level of fitness, wear suitable footwear and clothing, and carry food and water. It is also advisable to take the relevant OS map with you in case you get lost and leave the area covered by our maps.

Whilst every care has been taken to ensure the accuracy of the route directions, the publishers cannot accept responsibility for errors or omissions, or for changes in the details given. Nor can the publisher and copyright owners accept responsibility for any consequences arising from the use of this book.

If you find any inaccuracies in either the text or maps, please write or email us at the address below. Thank you.

First published in 2019 by:

Northern Eye Books Limited
Northern Eye Books, Tattenhall, Cheshire CH3 9PX

tony@northerneyebooks.com
www.northerneyebooks.co.uk

 @northerneyebooks

@northerneyeboo

For sales enquiries, please call 01928 723 744

Contents

South West Coast Path

Running for 630 miles from Minehead in Somerset, around the tip of Land's End and back to South Haven Point at the mouth of Poole Harbour in Dorset, the South West Coast Path is Britain's longest National Trail. Bordered by the Bristol and English channels and looking out to the open Atlantic, it encompasses some of England's most spectacular and wildest coastline, where the diversity of plant, animal and insect life can be stunning. The seas, coves and surrounding hinterland has been a dramatic setting for a gloriously rich history, which have inspired countless tales of romance, drama and intrigue.

This series of Top Ten Walks explores highlights along the way; showcasing its natural beauty, wildlife and heritage and provoking imagination. Who knows, you may be inspired to come back to tackle the complete trail.

Clovelly harbour shelters small fishing boats on the rugged North Devon coast

Somerset & North Devon Coast

Exmoor's majestic cliffs, secluded coves, wave-washed rocks and coastal woodland is a stunning prelude to the long distance trail. Further west are Devon's glorious beaches and an ever-more rugged coastline, battered by Atlantic surf. Large settlements are few, but occasional villages grew around coves where fishing and trade supplemented traditional farming. Nature complements the intrinsic beauty of this landscape; seabirds abound, while the unspoiled cliffs, native woodland, pasture and dunes support birds and butterflies — and you may even see red deer.

"Old England's counties by the sea
From east to west are seven;
But the gem of that fair galaxy
Is Devon, Devon, glorious Devon."

Sir Harold Boulton, *Lyrics to Glorious Devon*

TOP 10 **Walks:** Somerset & North Devon Coast

VICTORIAN HOLIDAYMAKERS AND ROMANTIC WRITERS began our love affair with this coast, popularising genteel resorts, viewpoints and rambles. The walks in this book will take you to some of the finest sections: from the Coast Path's iconic start at Minehead to the rugged cliffs and surf beaches of Bude. There are treacherous headlands that have wrecked countless ships, secluded smugglers' coves, shady glades and airy cliff tops with fantastic views. Altogether, it's an unmissable coast!

Minehead & Culver Cliff

Foreland Point

Woody Bay & Hunter's Inn

Bull Point & Morte Point

The South West Coast Path starts from Minehead's pretty harbour

Minehead & Culver Cliff

The initial leg of the South West Coast Path from Minehead onto Culver Cliff

What to expect:
Undulating woodland and heath paths, with a steep climb and long, zigzagging descent

Distance/Time: 7 kilometres/ 4½ miles. Allow 2½ to 3 hours

Start: South West Coast Path monument on Quay Street – several car parks in town

Grid ref: SS 971 468

Ordnance Survey map: Explorer OL 9: Barnstaple, Lynton, Minehead & Dulverton

Refreshment: The Old Ship Aground | 01643 703516 | www. theoldshipaground.com OR Echo Beach Café | 01643 709628

Walk Outline

From the striking map monument marking the start of the 630-mile South West Coast Path, the route contours the lower slopes of Culver Cliff before rising through woodland to Greenaleigh Farm. An easy path continues to ruined Burgundy Chapel before climbing along a wooded combe behind. The return takes a higher line across open heath and later through trees, dropping steeply back to the town.

The South West Coast Path

Although Minehead is commonly regarded as the 'start' of Britain's longest National Trail, the section crossing Somerset to North Devon was actually the last stage to be opened in 1978. It had been a mammoth project, with the first leg around Cornwall opening five years earlier. Much of its course follows centuries-old routes patrolled by Coastguards, but much new work was necessary in creating rights of way and viable paths across often difficult terrain. Today, maintenance is a never-ending task, combatting the effects of the weather and an estimated nine million walkers each year.

Map sculpture

Red deer

The Walk

1. From the striking **South West Coast Path monument**, situated towards the northern end of **Quay Street**, walk along the **promenade** with the sea on your right, passing the **harbour** and the **Old Ship Aground pub**.

The Bristol Channel boasts the second highest tidal range in the world, which can be up to 15 metres between high and low water. Following a series of major floods in the 1990s, Minehead's coastal defences were improved. Three kilometres of the seawall was heightened with a curved coping to deflect the power of the waves, the beach was replenished and groynes built to reduce erosion by longshore drift.

A footpath continues beside a **coastal park** before rising through trees across the steep slope of **Culver Cliff**. Ignoring a path off to Higher Town, shortly join a level path and then a tarmac drive leading to **Greenaleigh Farm**, which presides over small fields above **Greenaleigh Point**.

2. Keep going beyond the **farm buildings**, passing through a gate at the far end. The way, now signed to 'Burgundy Chapel', soon narrows to an undulating path through the **woods** and eventually leads to a **three-way signpost**. The overgrown ruins of Burgundy Chapel can be seen down to the right.

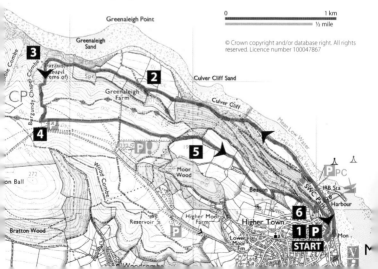

© Crown copyright and/or database right. All rights reserved. Licence number 100047867

Looking back through the trees towards Minehead

Although facing largely northwards, Somerset's coastline is some of the most wooded in the country, the long run of high cliffs providing shelter from the salt-laden prevailing winds, which blow from the south west. Much of it is dominated by broad-leaved native trees, in particular sessile oak and, as it has never been cleared for agriculture, is amongst the oldest continuous woodland in the country.

3. Go back to the junction and continue with the ongoing path, now signed to 'North Hill'. The way rises very steeply between the trees cloaking the flank of

Burgundy Chapel Combe. Breaking into more open ground, swing left in front of a **bench**, sited to take advantage of the view. The climb resumes, shortly reaching a junction. Once more on the **Coast Path**, keep ahead to another crossing of paths.

4. The way back is to the left along the lower of the two paths. Signed as a bridleway to 'Minehead', it passes below a **bench** to run across an **open heath** of furze and bracken, broken by occasional wind-stunted birch and rowan. *The view ahead is along the Bristol Channel towards*

Yellow gorse frames the view west from North Hill, Minehead

the distant promontory of Brean Down, off which are the small islands of Steep Holm and Flat Holm. Beyond a **concrete apron** at the end of a former tank run is another junction by a **wartime bunker**.

Large scale military activity dates back to the late 19th century when an infantry training camp was established on North Hill. The First World War saw thousands of new recruits passing through, housed largely in tents while they completed their training. During the Second World War, the area was used by British, Canadian and American troops for tank training, but little remains visible today apart from concrete roads and the bases of buildings.

5. Stick with the ongoing bridleway towards Minehead, which now gently descends into woodland. Reaching a diamond crossing keep ahead with the higher path; it soon curves to a junction. Go right through a gate to follow an old wall on your right. Emerging through a second gate, pass a **stand of pine** and continue at the top edge of pasture. Through a gate, cross a track and walk on across two more fields.

Eventually, past a **small stable**, look for a gate back into trees. Turn up left, and at the top swing right, soon winding to a junction. Go right again along a **sunken way** that leads to the end of a lane.

6. Cross to a footpath opposite signed to 'Minehead'. Watch for a path shortly doubling back left, which zigzags down the steep slope. Meeting the bend of another lane, cross to the ongoing path and carry on down. Ignore a crossing path, but just beyond, leave sharp left down steps. Below more zigzags, keep left and left again to emerge between houses onto **Quay Street** opposite the **Coast Path monument**, to complete the walk. ♦

Burgundy Chapel

Terraced into the steep, wooded hillside, the chapel may have origins in a hermit's cell or perhaps a votive chapel erected in thanksgiving for a safe return from an ill-fated expedition to France. Dunster Castle's records suggest it was there at the beginning of the 15th century. However, it may be much older. Today, little remains of the chapel other than a gable wall and carved doorway, but low walls beyond may have been a dwelling.

Sheep graze the grassy cliffs at Foreland Point

Foreland Point

Spectacular cliff scenery surrounding Devon's most northerly point

What to expect:
Undulating cliff paths with some steeper sections; the western path from Foreland Point is not recommended

Distance/Time: 9 kilometres/ 5½ miles. Allow 3 to 3½ hours

Start: Barna Barrow car park, Countisbury

Grid ref: SS 752 496

Ordnance Survey map: Explorer OL 9: Barnstaple, Lynton, Minehead & Dulverton

Refreshment: The Blue Ball Inn | 01598 741263 | www.blueballinn.com

Walk Outline

The walk begins across the moorland flank of Barna Barrow, passing onto the grazing of Kipscombe Hill. Leaving the fields, the way drops steadily below Desolate Farm to the Coast Path. The descent continues across coastal slopes through Chubhill Wood and Kipscombe Enclosure into Coddow Combe. After a there-and-back extension to Foreland Point, the route climbs behind The Foreland and returns by Butter Hill and past Countisbury's church.

The Foreland

The western flank of The Foreland isn't quite the highest point along Devon's coast, but it's certainly the most northerly. The lighthouse was commissioned in 1900, positioned to guide shipping along the channel to Bristol and the ports of South Wales. Although tucked low in the steep slope of Foreland Point, it is actually 67 metres above sea level and the light is visible from 33 kilometres away. Automated since 1994, the keepers' cottages are now a National Trust holiday let and while there's no general access to the compound, you can see it from the end of the track.

Elevated coast path

Stonechat

The view towards Lynmouth from Foreland Point

The Walk

1. Leave along a track between the bollards at the rear of the **car park**, branching right after a few metres onto a grass swathe. Keep right again where that shortly forks contouring the slope of **Barna Barrow**. Over an intersecting tarmac track, the onward path is signed to 'County Gate'. Stay by the left boundary, the path soon moving between gorse banks to join a track from **Kipscombe Farm**.

2. Meeting a tarmac track, bear right, but at the next sharp right-hand bend, bear off left above a **line of beech trees** sheltering the farm. Contour the flank of **Kipscombe Hill**, passing through three gates before losing height to a three way fingerpost.

3. Take the track through the gate, signed towards the 'Coast Path'. After 100 metres, watch for a waypost directing the path right and left across a **gully** to continue in a gradual descent across the heathery slope below the **Desolate farmstead**.

4. Reaching a signed junction, turn sharp left towards Lynmouth, now following the **Coast Path** back above the cliffs and into **Chubhill Wood**. Eventually, the path leaves **Glenthorne Cliffs** to meet a track, *where you might find a table furnished with a flask of hot water and the makings of tea, coffee and chocolate. This is Rodney's Honesty Café; serviced from the house, possibly glimpsed below you in the trees a little earlier on, which is thought to have been a 16th-century charcoal burner's cottage.* Joining the track, pass through a gate. Over a rise, bear right at a junction and head down to cross a **bridge** in **Coddow Combe**.

© Crown copyright and/or database right. All rights reserved. Licence number 100047867

Below the cliff here, just above the low tide mark is a fish weir, an 'L' shaped bank of shingle angled towards the sea. Any fish in the trap would be forced to the apex with the ebbing tide, where they could be collected in a net or basket. Such devices, constructed variously of wood or stone have been in use around the world since the Stone Age and over a dozen are known along this stretch of coast. Although of indeterminate age, those here are thought to be post medieval, some remaining in use into the 20th century.

5. The **Coast Path** and preferred route climb to the left, but you might first follow the ongoing track for another half mile to Devon's most northerly spot, **Foreland Point**. *There's a viewpoint overlooking the lighthouse and a row of cottages behind, built to house the keepers.*

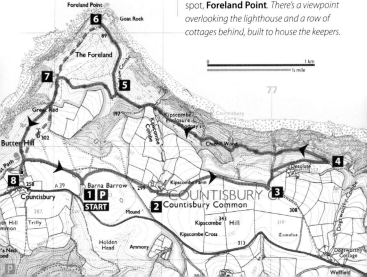

Looking west to Lynmouth and beyond from the OS 'trig' column on Foreland Point

6. Just before the end of the track, a narrow path climbs left to round the point and continue along the promontory's western flank to **Point 7**. However, a sign warns that it is steep, exposed and crosses loose scree, and it is not recommended, especially in wet or windy weather. Therefore, head back to **Point 5** turning right just before the bridge to resume the **Coast Path**. After an initial steep **flight of steps**, the gradient lessens into a steady plod that rises to a saddle behind **The Foreland**.

7. Go left towards Countisbury, now enjoying the view west to Lynmouth and Lynton. Just beyond **Great Red**, a dramatic gully sundering the cliff below, the path splits. The left fork climbs over **Butter Hill**, which offers a fine view along the North Devon coast, while the other contours its seaward flank. The paths come together after 400 metres at another junction above **Countisbury's church**; a lovely, simple building dedicated to St John the Evangelist. Although generally unlocked, the door needs a slight shove.

Rebuilt in the 18th and 19th centuries, this fine church has a much older feel, with a simple rood screen and carved pulpit, reading desk and lectern. It contains a framed ditty, attributed to Ted Ward: 'When

'ere I see a little church, I always pay a visit. So when at last I am carried in, The Lord won't say 'Who is it?'

The **Blue Ball Inn** lies beside the road just beyond.

8. Return to the junction above the church and bear right, following a path beside a wall. It curves across the southern slope of **Butter Hill** back to the **car park at Barna Barrow** to complete the walk. ♦

An epic rescue

It was 6:30pm on 12th January 1899 when the Lynmouth lifeboat was called to assist the Forrest Hall, foundering off Porlock. Huge waves prevented it launching, so the Louisa was hauled 13½ miles over Countisbury Hill and launched from Porlock the following morning. By nightfall, the stricken ship had been escorted safely to Barry from where the Louisa crew then rowed back to Lynmouth, arriving at 11:00am on the 14th.

Steep cliffs overlooking Woody Bay

Woody Bay & Hunter's Inn

Coastal woodlands, impressive cliffs, a splendid waterfall and the site of a Roman fortlet

What to expect:
Coastal and valley paths, some lane and two steady, sustained ascents

Distance/Time: 10.5 kilometres/ 6½ miles. Allow 3½ to 4 hours

Start: Hunter's Inn, National Trust car park (pay and display)

Grid ref: SS 655 480

Ordnance Survey map: Explorer OL 9: Barnstaple, Lynton, Minehead & Dulverton

Refreshment: Hunter's Inn | 01598 763230 | www.thehuntersinnexmoor

Walk Outline

The first leg follows the River Heddon down to the sea before winding inland to the sloping cliffs above Highveer Point. The climb continues along the coast, passing a picturesque waterfall before meeting a track above Woody Bay. After an uphill stretch on a quiet lane, the way back follows a delightful, easy track along the top of the cliffs, passing below the site of a Roman lookout post before turning in again along the beautiful Heddon Valley.

Luxury Resort?

Had things gone differently, Woody Bay might have become a fashionable resort. A successful Victorian solicitor, Colonel Benjamin Lake bought the Martinhoe estate, turning the manor house into a hotel and building a pier to attract passenger steamers. A golf course and sea bathing pool had been added by the time the railway arrived at Martinhoe Cross in 1898, with a branchline planned to Woody Bay. But two years later, Lake was accused of fraud, bankrupted and sentenced to 12 years in prison. The estate is now cared for by the National Trust.

Lime kiln at Heddon's Mouth

Dark green fritillary

The Walk

1. Out of the **car park**, follow the lane left, keeping left past the **Hunter's Inn**. Just after a bridge, turn off right along a track to 'Heddon's Mouth'. Beyond meadows it follows the **River Heddon** through a deep, wooded combe, later breaking from the trees below steep scree slopes. Remain on the left bank to **Heddon's Mouth**, where a 19th-century **limekiln** overlooks a stony beach.

2. Rough boulders act as stepping stones across the river mouth, but it is better to retrace your steps up the valley, crossing to the east bank over the first **bridge** you then come to. Continue upstream, the path gently rising and shortly reaching a junction, where 'Woody Bay' is signed back to the left. The way gains height

above the valley, eventually reaching the point above **Highveer Rocks**. There is a spectacular view across Heddon's Mouth, while to the east is Foreland Point.

3. The onward path climbs easily across a steep heather and furze slope before losing height to round the craggy nose of **Great Burland Rocks**. Further on, winding through trees, it passes the fern draped **waterfall** of **Hollow Brook**, which tumbles down the cliff at the back of a small combe. Later, through a gate, there is a glimpse ahead to **Martinhoe Manor**, set on an open terrace above the lower cliffs backing Woody Bay. Soon falling more steeply, the path ends at the sharp bend of a narrow lane.

4. Bear right, climbing steadily past a **cottage** for some 500 metres to meet the main lane. Go right and carry on more gently uphill past a small car park. Reaching a hairpin bend, leave the lane taking the broad track ahead, signed to 'Hunter's Inn'. The way runs more or less level for the next 1½

© Crown copyright and/ or database right. All rights reserved. Licence number 100047867

Looking east along the coast beyond Woody Bay

miles (2.4 kilometres), at first within rich woodland before breaking out onto open hillside. Beyond the trees, watch for a path detouring off left that climbs to **The Beacon**, the site of a Roman signal station on the rim of the cliff. Only traces of the perimeter earthworks remain, but it is a grand viewpoint. Return to continue with the main path below.

5. Eventually the path turns in above **Heddon's Mouth** and begins a long, gradual descent along the valley side. After swinging in around the side valley of **Hill Brook**, the way passes back into woodland. The track eventually runs out beside the **Hunter's Inn** to meet the lane. Keep ahead back to the **car park** to complete the walk. ♦

Hunter's Inn

By the 19th century, a farm cottage that originally occupied the site had become a local inn. However, in 1895 it was destroyed by fire, a not uncommon fate for thatched buildings. Part of Colonel Lake's scheme, it was rebuilt as an Alpine style hotel and immediately became a popular destination. Gone are the post-war days when weekly board was offered from 147 shillings (£7.35), but it remains an attractive centre for exploring the area.

The view along the coast from Grunta Beach towards Morte Point

Bull Point & Morte Point

Opportunities for time on the beach on this spectacular cliff walk, which includes a beautiful wooded combe

Distance/Time: 11 kilometres/ 7 miles. Allow 3½ to 4 hours

Start: Mortehoe village car park (pay and display)

Grid ref: SS 458 452

Ordnance Survey map: Explorer 139: Bideford, Ilfracombe & Barnstaple

Refreshment: The Ship Aground, Mortehoe | 01271 870856 | www.shipaground.co.uk OR The Grampus Inn, Lee | 01271 862906 www.thegrampusinn.co.uk

Walk Outline

Beginning in the attractive village of Mortehoe, the walk heads across country past Yarde Farm and Damage Barton before dropping into the Borough Valley. A wooded stream shows the way to the hamlet of Lee, where the route turns out to the coast behind Lee Bay. After a short stretch along a lane, it takes to the Coast Path, which follows an undulating course around Bull Point to Morte Point. The going is easier behind Grunta Beach before climbing back to Mortehoe.

Coastal erosion, Morthoe

Smugglers and Wreckers

There are few places along this coast that aren't steeped in tales of smuggling and wrecking, profitable sidelines for the rich and well-positioned as well as staving off hunger when times were hard for the needy. Around Morte Point, however, there was a darker side too, for it was said that shipwreck survivors were murdered to leave no witnesses. One of the most notorious wreckers was Elizabeth Berry of Mortehoe, who reputedly held drowning men underwater with a pitchfork; she was sentenced to hard labour for plundering a wreck in 1850.

'Wild' Exmoor ponies

The Walk

1. Leaving the **car park**, cross to **North Morte Road** opposite. Follow the street to its end in front of a gate to the **Bull Point Lighthouse**. Bear off right through a wooden gate into **Easewell Farm caravan site**. The track, signed to 'Lee', leads through the site.

2. Reaching the **facilities block**, keep ahead between the buildings, but watch for the footpath signed off left down steps past the original **farm buildings**. Drop beside a **small nature pool** and, through a gate, carry on beneath power cables to the end of a gravel path. Turn right and, following signs to 'Damage Barton', stay ahead, climbing between

hedges to a gate at the top. Keep going by the left field edge, passing forward to continue beside a second field and meeting a tarmac track at the far end.

3. Walk left around a bend and on to **Damage Barton**, winding up into a yard.

The manor dates back to at least the 12th century, possibly settled by a Norman knight whose descendants took the name Cutcliffe. They built the 16th-century farmhouse and held the farm for almost 500 years until its sale in 1922. The campsite complements the 580 acre farm which produces beef and lamb.

© Crown copyright and/or database right. All rights reserved. Licence number 100047867

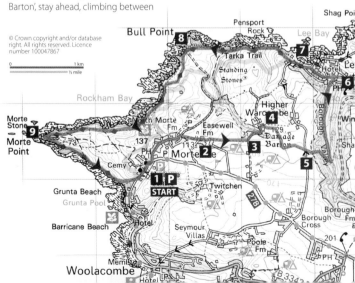

Rockham Bay and Bull Point from the Coast Path at Morthoe

Following a sign to 'Lee Bay', swing right and then keep ahead at an immediate junction past an **old barn**, the way now signed to 'Borough Woods'. At the end of the building, wind left, rising to a gate.

4. Instead of passing through, turn sharp right along a grass track. After 50 metres, leave at a waypost and climb left to a gate. Head away right across rough grazing, keeping right again at a signpost along a grass track. At a second signpost bear left to a third post, there passing through a gate into another field. Strike out along the field, closing with the left boundary. Halfway along, wind out over a gorsey hillock and drop to a small gate beyond. Go half-right across a final field to leave over a stile onto a narrow lane.

5. Over another stile opposite, bear slightly right across to find a stile into **Six Acre Wood**. The onward path falls steeply through the trees to a junction at the base of the valley. Go left towards Lee, passing through a kissing gate to continue along the valley. Eventually reaching a junction, walk right over a **bridge** and into the corner of a small meadow. Carry on at the right edge to emerge onto a contained path at the far side.

Bull Point Lighthouse warns shipping along this dangerous coast

6. The **Grampus Inn** lies just to the right, but the way back is left. Meeting a track, follow it on past **cottages** to come out onto a lane at **Lee Bay**.

7. To the left, it climbs steeply up from the **beach**. After 250 metres, watch for the **South West Coast Path** leaving onto **Damage Cliffs** between gateposts on the right. Over a rise, the path drops above **Sandy Cove**, where steps lead down to the beach. The path continues along the coast, losing and gaining height above the cliffs. There's another opportunity to access the beach opposite **Damagehue Rock** before climbing steeply once more and eventually passing behind the **Bull Point Lighthouse** enclosure.

Despite a local preference for Morte Point as being the more dangerous hazard on the peninsula, Morthoe's lighthouse was commissioned on Bull Point in 1879. However, they could not have foreseen the landslip there in 1972, which resulted in the light having to be rebuilt further inland.

8. Crossing the lighthouse access drive, the **Coast Path** carries on along the cliffs to **Rockham Bay**, where again there is a path to the beach. After a couple more sharp pulls, the path gradually descends to **Morte Point**.

9. Turning the point above low, fractured cliffs, there is a view ahead to Woolacombe's beaches. After some

300 metres, before a **seat above Windy Cove**, look out for the **Coast Path** dropping right down steps; it then runs easily above the low cliffs towards **Grunta Beach**. At the foot of a steep climb, go left up a grassy slope on the **Coast Path**, signed to 'Woolacombe via Combesgate Valley'. Carry on by the wall to the top below **The Old Chapel**. Emerge onto a lane and follow it left back through the village to the car park to complete the walk. ♦

Lee Bay

The slopes of converging valleys, too steep for farming, have allowed the survival of ancient woodland. Amongst the native species of oak, ash and hazel, you will also find beech, sweet chestnut and sycamore. The beach is particularly good for teeming rock pools, where in addition to barnacles, periwinkles and small crabs, there are anemones, mussels and whelks. There is plenty of seaweed too, including sea lettuce and laver, both of which can be eaten.

Croyde Bay is backed by a large dune system

Croyde Bay & Baggy Point

Two of North Devon's finest sandy beaches are linked on this splendid coastal walk over low cliffs

What to expect:
Tracks and coastal paths, only moderate climbs

Distance/Time: 7 kilometres/ 4½ miles. Allow 2½ to 3 hours

Start: Croyde Bay National Trust car park (pay and display)

Grid ref: SS 432 396

Ordnance Survey map: Explorer 139: Bideford, Ilfracombe & Barnstaple

Refreshment: Sandleigh Tea Room & Garden, Baggy Point | 01271 890930 | www.sandleighcroyde.com OR Putsborough Beach Café

Walk outline

Leaving the National Trust's car park at Croyde Bay, the route follows a farm track inland to climb the ridge of the peninsula and on at the edge of fields to Putsborough Sands. The return is along the Coast Path, which rises across Napps Cliff and on above gorse-clad slopes that fall to the rocky coast far below. Rounding the promontory, the path falls to the jagged rocks of Baggy Point before heading back at a lower level towards the broad expanse of Croyde Sand

A Special Place

Baggy Point was given to the National Trust in 1939 by the Hyde family. Living at Baggy House, they had long farmed the headland and, appreciating its beauty and diversity, did much to conserve the natural setting. The area is a designated SSSI for its geological interest: ice-borne boulders from Scotland's west coast and extensive wave-cut platforms. The coast is bright with wildflowers whose colour is at its best in late spring and early autumn, with kidney vetch, sea campion, tree mallow and autumn squill. Amongst the birds to look out for are stonechats and linnets whilst grey seals can sometimes be seen.

Baggy Point black ram

Tree mallow

The Walk

1. Turn left out of the **car park**, following the lane past the **Sandleigh Tea Room and Garden**. Leave just beyond, for a parallel footpath on the right. At its end, cross the lane to a track opposite that leads to **Orchard Farm**. Continue with the hedged track beyond, climbing gently between the fields.

2. Where the track eventually finishes at the entrance to a field, turn right along a narrower path, which runs on a **causey** beside a **stream**. Over a stile at its end, the track resumes. Follow it on, before long swinging right, but as it then later bends down to the right, keep ahead on a path signed to 'Putsborough Sands'.

3. Through a gate, keep going on a trod by the right-hand edge of hilltop pasture. Putsborough soon comes into view, the way then shortly passing a signpost in the hedge. Bear left towards a kissing gate in the corner, emerging onto a lane. Follow it down, passing through a **car park** to reach the **Beach Café** and the **sands** beyond.

4. When ready, head back to the kissing gate and climb away across the hillside to join a path that develops along the bottom edge of the field above the furze and blackthorn of **Napps Cliff**. The path continues onto the National Trust's land of **Baggy Point**, where ruby red Devon cattle are periodically grazed to control

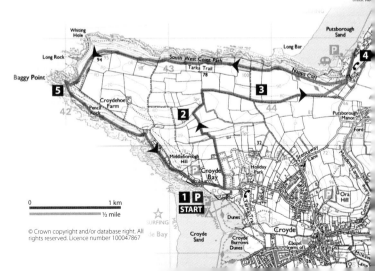

© Crown copyright and/or database right. All rights reserved. Licence number 100047867

Hardy Hebridean black sheep graze beside the coast path at Baggy Point

the spread of scrub. Eventually, the path rounds a shallow point above **Whiting Hole**. Walk on and past a **wreck post**, there bearing right to find a signpost marking a junction of paths. Go right with the **Coast Path**, dropping towards **Baggy Point**.

5. A path runs onto the finger of rock above the waves, but the way back is to the left along the southern flank of the headland. The path gradually loses height, levelling to pass **steps** down to the rocky beach. Through a gate by a **nature pond**, keep going, ultimately joining a drive. *Beside the path there is a massive bone from a whale that was washed onto the beach in 1915.* Follow the street ahead to return to the **car park** to complete the walk. ♦

Wreck post

The helplessness of being unable to assist distressed ships offshore prompted Cornishman Henry Trengouse to invent a rescue system for crews and passengers. His rocket could fire a line from either ship or shore and enable a breeches buoy to be rigged so that survivors could be winched safely to land. The 'wreck post' on the headland was set up by the coastguard for rocket crews to practice the rescue drill.

Clovelly's cobbled streets are too steep and narrow for wheeled transport

Clovelly & Mill Mouth

Woodland, cliffs and rocky beach feature on this splendid walk to one of Devon's prettiest coastal villages

What to expect:
Woodland, field and cliff-top paths, some steep climbs

Distance/Time: 11 kilometres/ 7 miles. Allow 3½ to 4 hours

Start: Brownsham National Trust car park (honesty box)

Grid ref: SS 285 259

Ordnance Survey map: Explorer 126: Clovelly & Hartland

Refreshment: New Inn, Clovelly | 01237 481303 | www.clovelly.co.uk OR The Red Lion, Clovelly | 01237 431237 | www.stayatclovelly.co.uk

Walk Outline

After descending along the wooded Brownsham valley, the way climbs out of the trees to follow a track past Court Farm to All Saints' Church. A lane leads to a stepped path down to Clovelly, an optional diversion. The way back picks up the Coast Path through Cliff Walk Wood and along the edge of a former Deer Park where another detour leads to a viewpoint above Blackchurch Rock. The onward route drops to Mouth Mill and its beach, before climbing above Brownsham Cliff. The final leg rises through Beckland Wood to the car park.

Clovelly's cobbled steps

Clovelly

Squeezed into a narrow rift between wooded cliffs, Clovelly's old cottages line a stepped, cobbled street that falls 120 metres to the tiny harbour at its foot. More than a hundred small mackerel and herring boats once sheltered here, their catches being carried out up the hill on the backs of donkeys. Part of the Clovelly estate — held by only three families since the 14th century — the village has changed little over the years. The streets are too narrow and steep for wheeled traffic, so goods are manhandled down from the end of the road on sleds.

Rooftop herring gull

The Walk

1. Leave the **car park** entrance and turn left down to **Brownsham Farm**. Walk through the yard then turn right in front of barns following a sign to 'Mouth Mill'. Stay with the main track, which winds gently downhill through **Brownsham Wood**.

Although partially planted with commercial Sitka spruce, Brownsham Wood contains an abundance of native trees such as oak, holly, ash, willow and birch. The neighbouring heath is culm grassland, where heavy, acidic soils encourage swathes of purple moor grass, rushes and orchids. Amongst the butterflies seen is the rare marsh fritillary.

2. At a junction towards the bottom, go ahead with the bridleway, crossing a **culverted stream** to a second junction. There turn left, but after 100 metres, leave right to climb away on a lesser track. Follow it up past a junction to a gate into a pasture. Walk on up the left edge and continue across another field, making for the far right corner. Exit through a gate and carry on along a track, which leads to **Court Farm**.

3. Keep going, now on a tarmac drive. Shortly reaching a junction by a **church** veer right (the entrance to the church and **Clovelly Court Gardens** are then over to the left). Walk out past a **lodge and estate gates** to a junction with the main lane.

© Crown copyright and/or database right. All rights reserved. Licence number 100047867

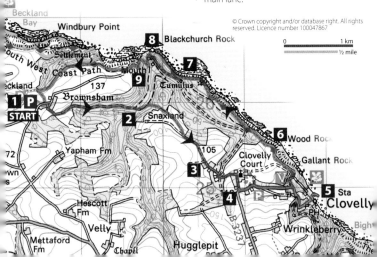

The ruined 18th-century lime kiln at Mouth MIll

4. Turn left, keeping with the lane beyond the end of the pavement (Clovelly car park and visitor centre are off to the right at that point). Reaching a bend by a small **residents' car park**, the onward route lies to the left, but to visit **Clovelly** itself, swing right and walk to the end from which a **cobbled street** drops steeply through the village to the harbour.

5. Climb back through the village and return to the bend by the residents' parking. Go right, but almost immediately, turn off left through a gate into the **Clovelly estate park**. Where the ongoing track then splits, fork right into woodland. Leaving the trees through a kissing gate, carry on at the right edge of **parkland**. Partway along, look out for a kissing gate taking the path back into the fringe of the woods and past a **small shelter** at the top of a short **flight of steps**.

6. A little further on, steps and another gate return you to the edge of the park, from which there is a view across to

Clovelly's iconic harbour seen from the steep steps above

Clovelly Court. Go right to yet another gate, which takes you back into the woods. Keep right at a junction and again at a fork to come upon an intriguing shelter, **The Angel's Wings**. Later meeting an estate track, walk right, but immediately branch right again with the **Coast Path**, rising to a kissing gate out of the trees onto **open heath**. The route ambles on over **Gallantry Bower**, passing a **viewpoint** at the far side before a gate. Returning to woodland, the way loses height to a junction.

7. To the right, a permissive path is signed to a viewpoint. Much less than the ½ mile indicated, the path rises easily away, passing a small **summer house** commanding a stunning view across the valley. Carry on to the **viewpoint**, which overlooks **Blackchurch Rock**.

8. Returning to the junction at **Point 7**, keep right and then right again to continue with the **Coast Path** down to **Mouth Mill** where there is access to the rocky beach. Follow the track as it swing left, but watch for the **Coast Path** then leaving down **steps** on the right. Wind across a **footbridge** and go left and then right to follow the path zigzagging steeply up the side of the valley.

9. Reaching the edge of grazing, follow the right boundary to a corner gate. Continue on a contained path, following the right-hand boundary beyond its end. Through a gate by a signpost, leave the Coast Path, going left towards Brownsham. The path dips into the trees. Keep ahead past a junction to a second one by a **bridge**. Go left through a gate and out of the woods. The path ahead returns to the **car park** to complete the walk. ♦

Mouth Mill

The old watermill, which once stood by the stream has disappeared and the impressive buildings now seen behind the beach are centred on an 18th-century limekiln, fed with limestone and coal shipped across the channel from the Welsh coast. The boulder beach is dominated by the massive Blackchurch Rock, a pyramidal stack of boldly striated sandstone and mudstone, folded over at a steep angle and pierced by two massive window-like openings.

Summer sea mist almost obscures the radome at Hartland

Hartland Point

A rugged and remote coastline that has claimed countless ships over the centuries

What to expect:
Field paths and tracks, with one or two steeper sections along the coast

Distance/Time: 9 kilometres/ 5½ miles. Allow 3 to 3½ hours

Start: East Titchberry National Trust car park

Grid ref: SS 244 270

Ordnance Survey map: Explorer 126: Clovelly & Hartland

Refreshment: The Point@Hartland outdoor café (Seasonal) | 07977 010463 | www.thepointhartland.co.uk

Walk Outline
Leaving East Titchberry the way follows the coast to Barley Bay before turning inland past Blagdon Farm. Dropping across a wooded valley, it climbs onto the next hill, there following a lane to Blegberry Farm. Crossing the fields to the Coast Path the route undulates north past Damehole Point to a waterfall, then climbs steeply beyond onto Blagdon Cliff to round the Hartland headland. The final section reverses the outward cliff-top route back to East Titchberry.

Hartland Point
During the 19th century, the cliffs south of Hartland were notoriously known as the Iron Coast because of all ships lost there. However, it was not until 1874 that a lighthouse was sited on the point. It was no less immune to the battering storms than the ships it sought to protect and a massive sea wall had to be constructed for its defence. Keepers' cottages were built alongside, but the steep, crumbling cliffs meant their vegetable garden was set a goodly distance away. The road to the lighthouse has now collapsed because of landslip and the automated light is serviced by helicopter.

Air traffic radome

Bottlenose dolphins

The Walk

1. Take the drive beside the **car park**, which leads past the thatched farmhouse and granary of **East Titchberry Farm**. Where the concrete ends, keep ahead through a gate on a hedged track. It shortly meets the **Coast Path** by a somewhat overgrown **viewpoint** above the inaccessible beach of **Shipload Bay**.

2. Follow the **Coast Path** left over a stile and on between tight hedges, *thick with blackberries and sloes in early autumn.*

Crossing into fields, carry on beside the boundary, the **geodesic radome of Hartland's air traffic radar station** an obvious landmark ahead.

A radar station was first established at Hartland during the Second World War, part of the Chain How Low system to give early warning of approaching low flying aircraft and shipping. From 1941, a Wireless Intercept (Y Station) was established to gather U-boat Enigma transmissions, which were forwarded to Bletchley for decoding. The station was re-commissioned during the Cold War as part of the ROTOR nuclear

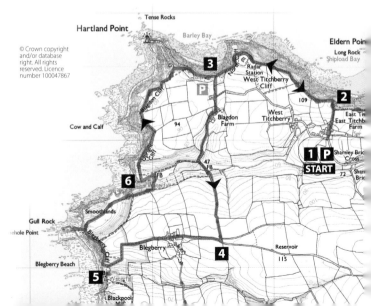

© Crown copyright and/or database right. All rights reserved. Licence number 100047867

Hartland Point Lighthouse with Lundy island on the horizon

early warning system, and is now operated as a radar station for both civilian and military air traffic control.

After passing a bench, where there is a better view back to Shipload Bay, the contained path resumes, skirting seaward of the radar complex and above cliffs backing **Barley Bay** before dropping to a track by a **car park** and the **Hartland outdoor café**.

3. Abandon the Coast Path, following the track inland. Keep ahead past a junction and on to **Blagdon Farm**. Wind past the buildings and through a gate to continue down at the edge of a narrow meadow. Stick with the ongoing track as far as a bend, there leaving left along a grass track that drops into bushes to ford a stream. A little further on cross a **footbridge** and then climb steadily away with the track onto **Blegberry Hill**.

4. Emerging onto a lane at the top, go right to **Blegberry Farm**. Walk on between the buildings, leaving along a grass track that shortly leads into a field. Go ahead to a signpost and drop left to find a kissing gate in the bottom boundary. A path slants down across the

Now a private house, Hartland Point Lighthouse was built in 1874

steep valley side, opening impressive views over **Blegberry Beach**.

5. Meeting the **Coast Path** walk right, gaining height above a rugged coast. Beyond the crest, the path falls sharply behind **Blegberry Cliff** towards **Damehole Point**. At the bottom, turn away from the sea at the edge of **Smoothlands**, a strangely flat valley, seemingly out of character to all around. Climb away at the far end and on at the edge of a field above a combe. Through a kissing gate, descend steeply to another gate at the bottom, crossing a bridge and bending above a stream towards the sea.

There is a small **waterfall** as the stream cascades over the edge to a pool behind the rocky beach.

6. The path swings uphill to continue along the top of **Upright Cliff**, so called because the rock strata have been tilted up on end. A little further on is a **memorial** to the *Glenart Castle*, a hospital ship that was sunk by torpedo some 20 miles offshore in 1918. The view opening ahead is to **Hartland Point**, where a lighthouse is perched on the end of the spit. The way runs to the compound gate of a **coastguard station**. There go right, joining a concrete path that leads down

to the lighthouse service road. Because of unstable cliffs and frequent rock falls, the track to the **lighthouse** is no longer safe and has been closed. Therefore, turn away from the locked gates and head up to the **car park** and **café**. Retrace your outward route past the **radar station** back to **East Titchberry** to complete the walk. ♦

Shipload Bay

The sheltered inlets of Devon's south coast offered countless safe landings for smugglers and so the excise men concentrated their efforts there. But smugglers on the savage north coast found it relatively unpatrolled and Shipload Bay was a frequented haunt, reached by a narrow path that meant contraband could be carried out on packhorses. The cliffs have since collapsed leaving the bay inaccessible, but it is a good place to watch for seals from the cliff top

The dramatic coastal waterfall at Hartland Quay

Hartland Quay & Stoke

An enjoyable ramble along a ragged, cliff-girt coast looking out to the Atlantic Ocean

What to expect:
Field paths and track, rugged coast path and moderate climbs

Distance/Time: 7 kilometres/ 4½ miles. Allow 2½ to 3 hours

Start: North Rocket House car park

Grid ref: SS 226 247

Ordnance Survey map: Explorer 126: Clovelly & Hartland

Refreshment: The Wrecker's Retreat, Hartland Quay | 01237 441218 | www.hartlandquayhotel.co.uk

Walk Outline

The walk starts out across The Warren, dropping to Dyer's Lookout and then turning inland above Abbey River to the church at Stoke. There's a detour to St Nectan's Well before following a track to Kernstone Cross. The way remains on tracks and a path to Speke's Mill Mouth, after which it runs north with the Coast Path to the foot of the valley crossed earlier. Tucking behind St Catherine's Tor, the route continues to Hartland Quay and then turns back to the car park.

Hartland Quay

The small harbour, built at Hartland in the 16th century, offered one of the few easy landings on this inhospitable coast and a busy settlement grew up. Coal and lime were landed to feed a limekiln and there were warehouses and a malthouse processing local grain. Despite damage during a gale in 1841, the pier was repaired, but trade then began to decline, exacerbated by agricultural depression and competition from the railway, which arrived in Bideford in 1855. Another storm in 1887 saw the end of the pier and the last trading ship left the beach in 1893.

Upright rock strata

Thrift or 'sea pinks'

The Walk

1. From the top entrance of the **car park**, go left, crossing the end of the lane to find the **South West Coast Path** leaving north beside the **Rocket House**. It follows the edge of **The Warren**, passing the impressive ruins of the **Pleasure House**.

The 18th-century tower stands on the site of a 16th- century building from which the surrounding warren was controlled. The large archway was apparently created so that the Orchard family, who then held Hartland Abbey, could drive their carriages in out of the elements to admire the sea view.

Towards the foot of the slope beyond, the path curves inland above the mouth of the **Abbey River**.

2. Abandon the **Coast Path** as it then drops to a **bridge**, and instead keep ahead up the **wooded valley**, the way signed towards 'Stoke'. Rising through the trees, the path breaks out at the edge of meadow. Reaching a fork at the far side, bear right, climbing beside the trees to reach a lane. However,

instead of joining it, go through the gate on the left to follow a parallel path that ultimately leads to the **churchyard of St Nectan's** at the edge of **Stoke**. Walk past the church to leave through a revolving **lychgate** at the eastern end of the churchyard, a rare survivor that retains its weighted closing mechanism. Join the lane ahead a short distance to find a path detouring off left to **St Nectan's Well**.

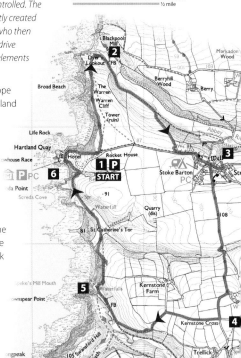

© Crown copyright and/or database right. All rights reserved. Licence number 100047867

Drifts of sea pinks decorate the coast in summer near Hartland Quay

3. Return to the lane and go briefly right before turning up beside **Church House**. The narrow lane rises from the village, degrading to a track that crests the shoulder of the hill and then falls past a **cottage** into the next valley. Climb steadily away to **Wargery Farm**. Follow the ongoing track out to **Kernstone Cross.**

4. Turn right along a farm lane. Later, keep left at a fork, descending more steeply to the end of the track by a **cottage**. The way continues through a kissing gate as a narrow path, losing height across the valley side to merge with a track along the bottom of the combe. Carry on to a **grassy terrace** overlooking the cliffs, down which the **stream** cascades in successive **waterfalls**.

5. The Coast Path climbs away, zigzagging onto the **headland** before dropping steeply down a long flight of **steps**. Curve right to a gate and continue across rough pasture around the foot of **St Catherine's Tor**. Through a gate, the way rises over more cliffs behind **Screda Cove**, then turns in to cross a stream before reaching the edge of a **car park** above **Hartland Quay**.

Rugged, much-folded cliffs at Hartland Quay

Although tales abound of wreckers luring ships onto Devon and Cornwall's rocky coast with false lights, there is no evidence that this ever happened. Indeed, visible shore lights would almost certainly have had the opposite effect warning captains to steer clear of land. Instead, wrecking was the opportunistic practice of salvaging cargo and even parts of the ship itself, washed onto the shore after coming to grief on the rocks. For remote and poor communities, this could be a significant windfall of goods that could be used or sold on. Folk saw the bounty as common property, but the local landowner often had rights too. There were frequent confrontations with the revenue men who *arrived on the scene, looking to impound goods that might be liable to duty, and as it was illegal to claim salvage if the crew still lived, there are tales of helpless survivors being abandoned for the loot. Nevertheless, local pragmatism was expressed in the prayer 'Oh please Lord, let us pray for all on the sea, but if there's got to be wrecks, please send them to we'.*

6. The **Wrecker's Retreat** and **museum** are down to the left, while the way back continues through a **car park** to the lane. Cross and climb away with the ongoing **Coast Path** which leads back to the **car park** beside the **Rocket House** to complete the walk.

Nearby Hartland Abbey's roots lie in an earlier collegiate church dedicated to St Nectan and founded around 1050 by Gytha, Countess of Wessex and mother of King Harold. It was re-founded a century later, under the Augustinian Order and continued as such until 1539, when it had the distinction of being the last monastery to be dissolved under Henry VIII. ♦

St Nectan's Church

The magnificent church at Stoke is known locally as the Cathedral of North Devon; its tradition dates from the 11th century, but the present building was begun around 1360. It has the second highest tower in the county and a beautiful painted and carved screen. It is dedicated to St Nectan, the son of a 5th-century Welsh king who reputedly had 24 brothers and 24 sisters. Inspired by St Anthony, he became a hermit and established his cell here beside a spring.

A path runs out along the aptly-named Higher Sharpnose Point

Morwenstow

An imposing coastline of abrupt rocky cliffs, a knife-edge point, sandy beach and eccentric clifftop retreat

What to expect:
Field paths and rugged coast path, some steep sections

Distance/Time: 6.5 kilometres/ 4 miles. Allow 2 to 2½ hours

Start: Rectory Farm Tea Room car park, Morwenstow

Grid ref: SS 205 152

Ordnance Survey map: Explorer 126: Clovelly & Hartland

Refreshment: Rectory Farm Tearooms and Garden, Morwenstow | 01288 331251 | www.rectory-tearooms.co.uk OR The Bush Inn, Crosstown | 01288 331242 | www.thebushinnmorwenstow.com

Walk Outline

Leaving Rectory Farm, the walk heads south across fields past the ancient settlements of Tonacombe and Stanbury to Eastway Manor. The way then falls along a valley to the coast above Stanbury Beach, there turning north to follow the Coast Path to Higher Sharpnose Point. After dropping across the mouth of Tidna Shute, there is a climb onto the cliffs, passing Hawker's Hut before turning inland back to Morwenstow.

Morwenstow

The parish is scattered across a number of farms, centred on the fine church, dedicated to both St John the Baptist and a Celtic saint, Morwenna, a sister of St Nectan. The present building dates from the 12th century, and has interesting Norman carving on the arches of the nave. On the north wall is the original figurehead from the brig *Caledonia*, wrecked off Sharpnose Point in September 1842. The sole survivor was Jersey man Edward Le Dain, who later sent a cow in gratitude for the care he received. The remainder of the crew were interred in a mass grave over which the figurehead was placed. A replica now marks the spot at the western end of the churchyard.

Morwenstow church interior

Gorse and heather

The Walk

1. Walk up beside the **car park** and **Rectory Farm** to go forward through a gate, the way signed to 'Tidna Valley'. Passing a **barn**, continue at the edge of pasture. Cross a track at the far side and keep going by the right hedge of another field. Negotiating more stiles at the corner, walk on to a kissing gate and head down into a **wooded valley**.

2. Meeting a crossing path at the bottom, go left to a waypost, there turning right over a bridged **stream**, the way signed to 'Tonacombe'. The ongoing path slants up to the right. Emerging through a couple of gates into a field, walk up by the hedge and then head straight across a second field into trees at the far side. Continuing forward, follow a short track and cross a drive emanating from the gates of **Tonacombe** into another field.

There is a glimpse of the early 16th-century fortified manor house buildings through the gateway as you pass. In Hawker's day both he and Charles Kingsley were visitors, and Kingsley's swashbuckling novel Westward Ho! *was partly written there.*

Keep going across a second field towards **Stanbury Farm**, beyond which the **dishes and antennae** of GCHQ are a prominent backdrop.

GCHQ's origins lie in the collection and decoding of military signals intelligence during the First World War, quickly enabling Britain to monitor virtually all German

© Crown copyright and/or database right. All rights reserved. Licence number 100047867

0 _____ 1 km

_____ ½ mile

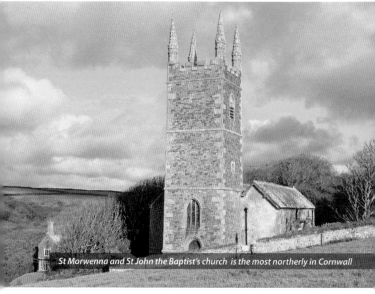

St Morwenna and St John the Baptist's church is the most northerly in Cornwall

strategic communication. GCHQ Bude, operational since 1974, occupies what was formerly RAF Cleave, a wartime airfield flying airborne targets for the various gunnery ranges around the South West coast. Mothballed after the war, the site was eventually developed as an intercept station to monitor both satellite communications relayed by the Goonhilly Down earth station, which opened in 1962, and telecommunications data passing through the transatlantic cables which land nearby. The station is a collaboration between GCHQ and the United States NSA (National Security Agency). Of course, the exact nature of the work is highly classified, but its activity impinges upon many aspects of national security, military activity, cyber security and major crime.

Exit by a small gate and stile just right of a **low barn** at the far side onto a track. Go left and then right through to a yard in front of the **manor house**. Leave left along a grass track into a field and bear half right, crossing to a stile in a shallow half corner. Maintain the line across a second field to the far corner.

Atlantic waves batter the rocky coast near Morwenstow

3. Through the gap, turn right and head away from the lane beside the hedge. Walk on in the field beyond into the deepening fold of a valley to find a stile hidden in the trees. Over a **bridge**, go left through a gate, descending through gorse to a kissing gate into a field. Carry on down the edge, dropping out at the bottom corner onto the bend of a grass track. Keep going ahead, passing through a gate and on towards the coast above **Stanbury Mouth**, where there is access to the **beach**.

4. Approaching the coast, watch for the **South West Coast Path** rising away to the right. After a steep climb, there is a pleasant run along the cliffs towards **Higher Sharpnose Point**. Losing height the path reaches a ruined **coastguard shelter** looking out along the knife-edge promontory.

5. The ongoing path swings in front of the shelter, opening views to the north. The way falls to the base of **Tidna Shute**, bending left and right to cross its **stream** before climbing away. Entering pasture at the top, bear left to regain the cliffs, shortly passing through a gate. Some 50 metres beyond, keep an eye open for a stepped path leaving on the left, which drops to **Hawker's Hut**. Go back to the clifftop and walk just a little further to pass through

a gate opening. Leaving the **Coast Path** now, head inland at the top edge of successive fields, until a track develops that takes you back to the **car park** to complete the walk.

Morwenstow's 13th-century church is well worth exploring. Inside are fine Norman carvings including a row of alternating bearded men and beaked creatures. ♦

Reverend Robert Stephen Hawker

Hawker came to the parish in 1834 and is remembered for his efforts in saving and caring for shipwrecked mariners. He also introduced harvest thanksgiving as a church festival and wrote poems, the best known perhaps being the Ballad of Trelawney with its refrain, "Here's twenty thousand Cornish men, Will know the reason why!". The tiny hut atop the cliffs was his 'man cave', where he gazed out upon the sea for inspiration.

Atlantic breakers pound Duckpool beach at sunset

Coombe Valley

Stunning coastal scenery and superb sandy beaches coupled with a delightful wooded combe

What to expect:
Steady rises along inland woodland paths, occasional steeper climbs on undulating coast

Distance/Time: 10.5 kilometres/ 6½ miles. Allow 3¼ to 4 hours

Start: Duckpool Bay National Trust car park (honesty box)

Grid ref: SS 201 116

Ordnance Survey map: Explorer 126: Clovelly & Hartland

Refreshment: Margaret's Rustic Tea Garden, Northcott Mouth (Seasonal) | 07747 537564 OR Sandymouth Café | 01288 354286 | www.sandymouth.com

Walk Outline

Following the lane inland, the route takes paths along Coombe Valley before crossing the stream and climbing through Stowe Wood to Stowe Barton. Over a lane, it continues across open fields, eventually descending below Dunsmouth Farm to meet the coast at Northcott Mouth, where there is a fine beach and refreshment. The return joins the Coast Path north, the cliffs becoming higher beyond Sandy Mouth before finally dropping back to Duckpool.

Ship's boiler, Duckpool beach

Duckpool

A shingle bank across the beachhead at Duckpool blocks the stream's flow from the valley and one story claims the pond's name derived from its use as a baptismal pool by early Baptists. Coincidentally, there are ducks here, too. Roman traders took advantage of its good access and fine sandy beach, and a prehistoric settlement has been identified on a hill above Coombe Valley. Behind the beach, archaeologists discovered hearths and Romano-British objects, including coins that suggest silver refining and possibly the stamping of coinage, was undertaken here.

Heron on the shore

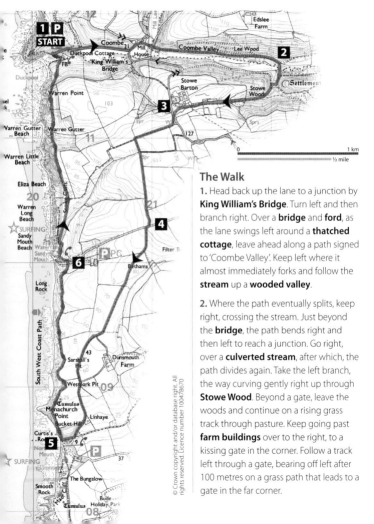

© Crown copyright and/or database right. All rights reserved. Licence number 100478670

The Walk

1. Head back up the lane to a junction by **King William's Bridge.** Turn left and then branch right. Over a **bridge** and **ford**, as the lane swings left around a **thatched cottage**, leave ahead along a path signed to 'Coombe Valley'. Keep left where it almost immediately forks and follow the **stream** up a **wooded valley**.

2. Where the path eventually splits, keep right, crossing the stream. Just beyond the **bridge**, the path bends right and then left to reach a junction. Go right, over a **culverted stream**, after which, the path divides again. Take the left branch, the way curving gently right up through **Stowe Wood**. Beyond a gate, leave the woods and continue on a rising grass track through pasture. Keep going past **farm buildings** over to the right, to a kissing gate in the corner. Follow a track left through a gate, bearing off left after 100 metres on a grass path that leads to a gate in the far corner.

Striking, stratified red rocks at Northcott Mouth beach

3. Cross a lane to a track opposite signed to 'Northcott Mouth'. Swing right, passing through a gate to continue at the edge of a field. Reaching a junction, go left and follow the edge of three fields to meet another lane.

4. Take the **hedged track** opposite. At a fork bear right and carry on as another track shortly joins, descending gently across successive open fields from where there is a grand view along the coast to Tintagel and beyond. After a mile/1.5 kilometres, the track leads past **Margaret's Rustic Tea Garden** and

winds out to the coast at **Northcott Mouth**, where low tide reveals a fine sandy beach.

The inter-tidal rocks and pools offer a tempting diversion for exploration. Amongst things to look out for are coral-like growths attached to the rocks. They are small reefs built by colonies of the honeycomb worm, each tube-like hole housing an individual worm. The clusters of tubes are constructed from sand and shell particles cemented together, and at high water, the worms extend feathery tentacles to feed on passing plankton.

The broad stream valley above Duckpool

5. Walk onto the head of the beach and turn right across a **stream** to the foot of **steps** which climb steeply onto the cliff behind.

Occasionally visible at low tide in the sand off Menachurch Point are the remains of the SS Belem. A German cargo vessel interned by the then neutral Portuguese, it was pressed into allied service after Germany declared war on Portugal in 1916. In November 1917, it was returning to Cardiff with a cargo of iron ore, keeping close to the coast as it approached the Bristol Channel to avoid the U-boats which regularly patrolled the area. Misjudging its position in thick fog, it grounded on the rocks, and

although the crew were brought to shore using a rocket-fired line and breeches buoy, the ship broke its back before it could be towed off.

The **South West Coast Path** undulates on, high above the sands, eventually dropping to **Sandy Mouth**, where there is another **café**.

6. Cross the track diagonally left, following Coast Path signs to a gate. Ignore the track then off right and head on across pasture, curving right to find a **bridge spanning a gully** that twists down to the coast. The path then bends right to rise along the valley side to a

waypost at the top. Branch off left over a rise to continue along the undulating cliffs above **Eliza Beach** and **Warren Little Beach**. A final challenge is presented by **Warren Gutter**, the path rising beyond over **Warren Point** before a final long, slanting descent into the flat-bottomed valley behind **Duckpool**. Over a **bridge**, go left back to the **car park**, to complete the walk. ♦

A swashbuckling life?

A contemporary of Sir Francis Drake and cousin of Sir Walter Raleigh, Sir Richard Greville held estates in Devon and the manor here at Stowe. He led a colourful life as a sailor, privateer and explorer, establishing colonies in Ireland and the New World. He met his end fighting the Spanish off Flores in the Azores, his ship the Revenge *hopelessly outnumbered by the Spanish. His crew eventually surrendered and Greville died shortly after from his wounds.*

Useful Information

Visit Somerset and North Devon

Three official tourism websites cover the area, detailing everything from accommodation and special events to attractions and adventure: **www.visitsomerset.co.uk**, **www.visitdevon.co.uk** and **www.visitcornwall.com**

AONBs and National Parks

To learn more about the Exmoor National Park and the coastal Area of Outsanding Natural Beauty, see: **www.exmoor-nationalpark.gov.uk, www.northdevon-aonb.org.uk** and **www.cornwall-aonb.gov.uk**

Selected Tourist Information Centres

The main TICs provide free information on everything from accommodation and transport to what's on and walking advice.

Clovelly – 01237 431781
Combe Martin – 01271 883319
Barnstaple – 01271 346747
Bideford – 01237 477676
Bude – 01288 354240
Hartland – 01237 441916
Ilfracombe – 01271 863001
Lynton & Lynmouth – 01598 752225
Minehead – 01643 702624
Porlock – 01643 863150
Woolacombe – 01271 870553

Rail Travel

There's a station at Barnstaple. National Rail Enquiries 08457 484950 or **www.nationalrail.com.uk**

Bus Travel

Many places along the north coast are served by bus: **www.travelinesw.com**

Camping

This is a popular area for camping, with many sites owned by or affiliated to the Camping and Caravanning Club: 024 7647 5426; **www.campingandcaravanningclub.co.uk**